Anonymous

American Slavery

Demonstrations in Favor of Dr. Cheever, in Scotland

Anonymous

American Slavery
Demonstrations in Favor of Dr. Cheever, in Scotland

ISBN/EAN: 9783744732758

Printed in Europe, USA, Canada, Australia, Japan

Cover: Foto ©ninafisch / pixelio.de

More available books at **www.hansebooks.com**

American Slavery.

DEMONSTRATIONS

IN FAVOR OF

DR. CHEEVER, IN SCOTLAND.

LETTER OF SYMPATHY FROM DISTINGUISHED
CLERGYMEN AND OTHER GENTLEMEN.

SPEECHES

AT MEETINGS IN EDINBURGH AND GLASGOW, BY

DRS. CANDLISH, GUTHRIE, ALEXANDER, BUCHANAN,
AND SMYTH.

AND A STATEMENT OF

DR. CHEEVER'S CASE, BY REV. H. BATCHELOR.

LETTER OF DR. GUTHRIE TO THE PRESBYTERIAN.

New-York:
JOHN A. GRAY, PRINTER & STEREOTYPER, 16 & 18 JACOB ST.
1860.

EDINBURGH, 19 January, 1860.

REV. DR. CHEEVER:

REV. DEAR SIR: We, whose names are hereto adhibited, Ministers of the Gospel, Office-Bearers, and others belonging to the evangelical denominations of this City, desire to give expression to our Christian sympathy with you in the unequal contest in which you are engaged with the abettors of Slavery. We have no doubt that you have been raised up in the providence of God to witness for his truth, regarding the rights and privileges of our colored brethren held in cruel bondage.

The struggle you are honored to maintain, of "Right against Might," is but a part of the prolonged conflict which we and our fathers waged with the pro-slavery party of this country, and which closed, as you know, in the glorious emancipation of our slaves, and the extinction of the accursed traffic in human beings throughout all the colonies of Great Britain.

Our experience assures us that, whoever stands forward as the asserter of universal freedom, must be prepared for the most determined opposition of all who are interested in the trampling down this the most sacred and inalienable birthright of the human family. But our experience also assures that, until the ministers of Christianity courageously assume the post of leaders on the side of freedom in the contest, and fearlessly assert God's truth against the supporters and apologists of Slavery, the great sin against which you are contending will never be abolished.

You have been called to suffer shame and wrong for the part you have acted in this good cause. We doubt not you laid your account with this at the outset, and counted the cost ere you plunged into the strife. We honor you for your manliness; we sympathize with you in the trials you have endured; and our earnest desire is, that you should hold by the position you have assumed. You are the advocate of a cause dear to the heart of the nations of the brave and the free—a cause which, however maligned and betrayed, must triumph in the end. We must cease to have faith in prophetic vision before we can despair of the universal acknowledgment of the position so truly set forth in the American Declaration of Independence, yet so pertinaciously trampled upon—namely, "that all men are born free and equal."

We are assured that we speak the sentiments of this great nation itself in the expression we have conveyed to you of our respect and sympathy. Our prayers ascend that victory may speedily crown the peaceful agitation you have awakened, by the United States proclaiming freedom to every slave on her soil, when the beautifully just and true sentiment now cited shall no more be her reproach, but her glory.

We hope shortly to be able to convey to you a more substantial expression of our interest in your cause. We send this in the mean time, that you may be assured of our fraternal sympathy, and may be encouraged and assisted thereby to persevere in the good work in which you have embarked.

We rest, Reverend Sir, for ourselves and many others who in like manner sympathize with you,

    Most truly yours, in Gospel bonds,
F. BROWN DOUGLAS, Lord Provost of Edinburgh,
ROBT. CANDLISH, D.D.,
W. LINDSAY ALEXANDER, D.D.,
WM. GLOVER, D.D.,
ANDREW THOMSON, D.D.,
THOMAS GUTHRIE, D.D.,

James Begg, D.D.,
H. Wellwood Moncreiff, Bart.
James Robertson, Newington Church, (U. P.,)
G. D. Cullen, A.M.,
J. Wm. Watson, Dublin Street Church,
W. C. Anderson, Major-General Royal Artillery,
Jno. Millar, Merchant, 13 York Place,
J. Burn Murdock, Jr., Advocate,
W. D. Dickie, 19 George Street,
D. McLaren, Newington House, Ex-Lord Provost,
John Melville, Knt., 15 Heriot Row, Ex-Lord Provost,
J. Begbie, M.D.,
Thomas Cleghorn, Advocate, Sheriff of Argyleshire,
John Maitland, Accountant to the Court of Session,
M. W. Macdonald Hume, of Nine Wells,
J. H. A. Macdonald, Advocate,
Fred. Maitland Heriot, Advocate-Deputy,
A. W. Campbell,
James Bonar,
James Miller, F.R.C.E., Prof. of Surgery in the University of Edinburgh,
Chas. Cowan, of Valleyfield, late M.P. for Edinburgh,
P. Davidson, Minister,
Alexander Davidson, M.A.,
James Davidson, M.A,
Cumberland Hill, Elder,
A. Davidson, Elder,
Robert Johnstone, LL.B.,
William Gillespie, U. P. Min., Chalmers Close Ch.,
Adam Pearson, 13 Arneston Place, Counselor,
John Coghlan, Missionary, Edinburgh,
John Writon, of Darnick Tower,
W. Rinton, Prince Street,
W. H. Billing, 22 Dean Terrace,

Rev. Thos. Finlayson, Rose Street U. P. Church,
James Duncan, Writer to Her Majesty's Signet, Elder,
Andrew Williamson, Merchant, Leith, Elder,
James Brydon, Merchant, Edinburgh, Elder,
James Richardson, Merchant, Edinburgh, Elder.
George Henderson, Elder,
D. J. Robertson, City Chamberlain, Elder,
Andrew Fyfe, S.S.C., Elder,
W. M. Begbie, Rector of Burns Place School, Elder,
George Gliss, Elder,
Wm. Lyon, Elder,
John Henderson, Elder,
James Cameron, Member Rose Street,
Wm. Calderwood, Elder,
Wm. Anderson, Elder,
Wm. Duncan, Elder,
Wm. Paterson, Elder,
George Alston, Elder,
Thomas Hopper, Elder,
W. Luckie, 11 Carlton Terrace, Banker,
J. W. MacGregor, Assistant to Dr. Glover, Greenside, Edinburgh,
N. Snody, 26 Gayfield Square, Edinburgh,
J. S. Wardlaw, A.M., Missionary L. M. S.,
D. T. K. Drummond, St. Thomas Epis. Ch., Edinburgh,
Will Lillie, 1 Newington Terrace,
William Gillon, 5 Fingal Place, Edinburgh,
Wm. Stacey Chapman, B.A., Charlotte Chapel,
W. K. Tweedie, D.D.,
J. Gibson Thomson, Elder,
Chas. Jas. Kerr, Elder,
George Nicholson, Elder,
Robert You, Elder,
A. K. Morison, Deacon,

John Croall, Deacon,
John Gulland, Deacon,
Wm. Reid, Minister of Lothian Road United Pres. Ch.,
Jno. Reid, Elder, " " "
John Greig, Elder, " " "
James Turnbull, Elder, " " "
William Brown, " " " "
Robt. Lawson, " " " "
Hugh Kilpatrick, Elder Lothian Road Church,
George B., " " " "
James Lawson, " " " "
Robert Hume, " " " "
Archibald McPherson, " " " "
Thomas Dick, " " " "
Thomas Dawson, " " " "
James Law, " " " "
Rev. John Kirk, 17 Greenhill Garden, Brighton St. Ch.,
J. Young, 29 Minto Street,
James Dippie, 1 Farquharson Place,
J. G. M. Williamson, 4 Fingal Place,
Alex. Cromar, 14 Upper Gray Street,
W. Young, M.D.,
N. O'Brien, Major, Edinburgh,
Harry Armour, Edinburgh,
John Horsburgh, Edinburgh,
James Leishman,
George Johnston, D.D.,
William Swan, 7 Hope Crescent,
William Pulsford, Minister, ⎫
John A. Fullarton, Deacon,   ⎪ Signed on behalf of
Thomas Callam, Deacon,   ⎬ the Church and Con-
Wm. Anderson, Deacon,   ⎪ gregation of Albany
George Cullan,   ⎭ Street Chapel.
William Peddie, D.D., (U. P.)

AMERICAN SLAVERY.

DR. CHEEVER'S POSITION AND JOHN BROWN'S EXECUTION.

PUBLIC MEETING IN EDINBURGH.

A large and influential public meeting took place on Thursday afternoon, in the Queen street Hall, convened for the purpose of expressing sympathy with the Rev. Dr. Cheever under the painful circumstances which that eminent divine has lately been called on to occupy with reference to slavery. Among those on the platform were the Lord Provost, Sir James Forrest, Sir John Melville, Rev. Dr. Candlish, Rev. Dr. Guthrie, Rev. Dr. Alexander, Rev. Mr. Cullen, Rev. Jonathan Watson, Rev. Mr. Graham of Newhaven, Rev. Mr. Pulsford, Dr. Greville, Dr. Russell, Mr. J. F. Macfarlan, Mr. H. D. Dickie, Counselor Fyfe, Mr. Cruickshank, Mr. Burn Murdoch, Jr., Mr. Snoedy, etc., etc. On the motion of Sir John Melville, the Lord Provost was called to the chair. The meeting having been opened with prayer by Mr. Pulsford,

The Lord Provost briefly stated the object of the meeting, which, he was happy to say, was not of a very usual character in Edinburgh. They were called together to express sympathy with a Christian minister in very peculiar circumstances; a man well known to the people of this country by his writings, and by his admirable illustrations, he believed the best of all others, of John Bunyan, and one who at the present time needed all the sympathy and any encouragement that could be given him. [Applause.] After remarking that it was by no means uncommon or extraordinary for the people of this country publicly to express their approbation or disapprobation of events in other lands, in proof of which he instanced the case of the Jew boy, Mortara, and the remonstrance they made in the case of those who were tried and imprisoned in foreign countries for reading the Bible, his lordship went on to express his astonishment that, in the United States of America, which vaunted so loudly of their freedom, civil, political, and religious, there should not only be a toleration of the abominable system of slavery, but that when Christian men opened their mouths to condemn it, they were not only not sympathized with, but were themselves condemned by public opinion.

Dr. CANDLISH, who was received with loud cheers, then addressed the meeting. After referring to the private manner in which the movement in behalf of Dr. Cheever had been hitherto gone about, and to the drawback necessarily incident to this, he said, that if the cause with which that eminent man was identified had been brought before the community of Scotland in the way in which such cases ordinarily were, it was his impression that the steam would have been up long ago, and a national enthusiasm would have been kindled. It was, however, now made abundantly plain that Dr. Cheever was suffering for his faithfulness in advocating the cause of emancipation, and that the movement now making on his behalf on this side of the Atlantic had his thorough sanction, and that of the large and overwhelming majority of his congregation. Having adverted to the attempt made, during his absence on sick leave, by some of the wealthier portion of Dr. Cheever's congregation, to get him to resign in consequence of his preaching on the subject of slavery, and to the failure of this attempt, Dr. Candlish next stated that these parties now withheld all support from the congregation, and observed that the tendency, if not the design, of all their proceedings was, that Dr. Cheever should be shut up to the necessity of abandoning the prominent position which he held as pastor of the Church of the Puritans in New-York. And it is (continued Dr. Candlish) for the purpose of enabling Dr. Cheever to continue in this position, and to continue in it without the risk of being troubled from year to year, that the movement is made by his friends and his congregation, and that we are asked to aid in it. The object of that movement is not merely to provide for the passing year, but to provide such a sum as shall enable the Church of the Puritans to clear themselves of all encumbrances, and so to maintain its position as a church, in whose pulpit Dr. Cheever thunders his anathemas against all sin, and the sin of slavery among others. [Cheers.] I do trust that, now that this cause has been fairly brought under our notice in this public way, we shall give to it our most cordial sympathies, and shall, with one heart and one hand, combine to support Dr. Cheever in his influential position. [Cheers.] Among other questions, this has sometimes been asked: Is it not strange that in such a city as New-York, and in such a country as America, and especially in the North, where, although public sentiment is to a large extent, I fear I may say debauched, by the political entanglements in which the North is involved with the South—where, notwithstanding this, there is notoriously a very large and influential anti-slavery party—how comes it, some say, that Dr. Cheever is not sustained by the friends of the anti-slavery cause in the States of America themselves? and how comes it that when, as is alleged, there are a good many ministers—not a very large proportion, for even those most favorable to the clergy of America admit that it is a very small proportion—but while there is a considerable body of ministers in the Northern States of America who are avowedly anti-slavery, and who make no hesitation about declaring their sentiments—how comes it that Dr. Cheever, in particular, should suffer more than they do? I confess I had some difficulty on this very point myself when the matter was first brought under my notice; but on getting information upon it from the American newspapers, not from those favorable to Dr. Cheever, but chiefly from one newspaper rather hostile to him, and more especially from reading Dr. Cheever's own book, "God against Slavery," I got the enigma or riddle thoroughly solved, for I found that the peculiar offense of Dr. Cheever consists, not in holding abstractly anti-slavery views, or in propounding them, but that his peculiar offense is that he launches forth, with an eloquence worthy of the old masters of oratory in Greece—with an eloquence, I would almost say, rivaling the denunciations of the prophets, in so far as uninspired eloquence can rival that of inspiration—he sets himself not merely to the general advocacy of emancipation, but he sets himself tooth and nail against the measures of the American Legislature sanctioning, promoting, and extending slavery; he sets himself practically to work against the Kansas atrocity, against the Fugitive Slave Law; he sets himself against every form by which the Legislature of America has been abetting and encouraging the evil; and he does so in the way just of strong and pointed appeal to the consciences of all American citizens, calling upon them to exercise their political franchise, as in the sight of God, and against this abominable sin. [Loud cheers.] This is his special offense; and here, I believe, he stands almost alone among the ministers of America. I believe he might have gone on denouncing slavery in the abstract as long as he chose, and in pronouncing anathemas against it, and preaching up emancipation in the abstract; but here he comes home to men's bosoms, to men's business, and to men's purses—he comes home to them as citizens, and he calls upon them to consider that they are responsible for the enormous sin which the Legislature of the States is committing, in not merely tolerating slavery where it exists, but in building for it bulwarks to preserve and perpetuate the institution, and in opening up new fields, through bloodshed and violence, for the entering in and triumphing of it on the free soil of the States of America. [Loud cheers.] This is the head and front of Dr. Cheever's offending, and we will at once see that this places him in a somewhat peculiar position.

Dr. Candlish then referred to three classes of anti-slavery men in America; first, those who bear a milk-and-water testimony; second, those who, opposed as they may be to slavery, can not be expected to enter very cordially into a measure bearing even in the slightest degree on ecclesiastical organization, or upon the maintenance of a minister belonging to another church; and third, those who, opposed to slavery out and out, and more or less distinctly on Christian grounds, take up the position that they ought to enlighten the public mind on the subject, but ought not to interfere either by force—as John Brown had been doing —or by any thing approaching political agitation, which unquestionably was the offense of Dr. Cheever; and said that none of these classes could be expected to sympathize much with Dr. Cheever in his present position, or in the effort now making to secure his position in the Church of the Puritans. Now, there can be no question (continued Dr. Candlish) that Dr. Cheever stands out, I don't say as the martyr John Brown, but as a confessor of this great principle—and I hold it to be a great principle—that the opponents of slavery in America are bound to make their opposition to it tell on the hustings—[cheers]—that they are bound to make their opposition to slavery tell through the ballot-box—that they are bound to testify to their fellow-citizens every where that those who hold the reins of power, and those who, in the last resort, rule their country, are responsible for the measures that are drawing down upon America, if America pause not, the righteous indignation of Him who will have all men to be free. [Loud cheers.] Having made this explanation as to Dr. Cheever's position, will you allow me just to advert for a little to Dr. Cheever's way of advocating the anti-slavery cause. I thoroughly agree with Dr. Cheever, that all men in America who hold the truth on this subject are bound to be energetically active, not merely testifying, but acting and calling upon all their fellow-citizens to act too. Why, some years ago, there might be some pretense for saying that it was enough for anti-slavery men in America to bear testimony against slavery, to circulate information on the subject, and to endeavor, through the press and otherwise, to leaven the public mind with sound views; there might be some shadow of pretense for this some years ago, when, as it seemed, the line was drawn, and slavery was limited and pent up—pent up within a certain space, within which there was some prospect that it might die out in course of time—that enlightened views might come to prevail, and that slavery might expire under the influence of truth; but the course of things has been entirely and altogether altered since slavery has taken the aggressive—since slavery in America, not content with being tolerated in the places to which it was restricted, became aggressive in the worst sense—aggressive not merely in a lawful way, through the Legislature, in procuring the passing of such infamous acts as the Fugitive Slave Law—but aggressive by the bowie-knife and the rifle, [cheers,] as witness a senator shot on the floor of the Senate; aggressive, moreover, by force of arms, as witness the atrocities and illegal proceedings that have disgraced the province of Kansas. [Renewed cheers.] And, worst than all, these movements of slavery, so far from having been checked by the general Legislature of America, are getting the countenance of that Legislature, so that such enormities as those of Kansas, confessedly illegal as they are, are really supported and upheld by the whole force of the United States army. [Cheers.] Now, in these circumstances, the case has been altogether altered; and as to any hope which might have been entertained of the evil being pent up in certain localities, and silently and gradually disappearing under the progress of enlightened views, these must be given up; for we have here a hostile power—hostile to liberty, hostile to God, and hostile to man—raising itself in increased strength, drawn forth, not from above, but from beneath, bursting the bounds within which it was hoped it had been fettered, and coming forth to pollute the free air of the North, and to debauch men's minds all over America, and by sheer force of arms, and by the sheer force of importunity in the Legislature, threatening to break up the Union, and to compel the free soil of America to be stained by the curse of slavery. [Cheers.] The time has now, therefore, fully come for Christian men and Christian churches, acting upon this belief, and especially in the whole of the Northern States, and for awaking to a sense of their responsibility in connection with the exercise of their political rights. Dr. Candlish here referred to Dr. Cheever's volume, "God against Slavery," and stated that, after having read it, he found that there was no ground for the supposition that Dr. Cheever entertained ultra or extreme views on the subject of slavery, or advocated the cause in an injudicious spirit, but heartily subscribed to every sentence and word in this noble work, as he thought it was fitted to carry conviction, and ultimately to enlist the enthusiasm of every friend of the Gospel, as well as of every friend of the slave. He further stated, that a considerable portion of the volume was taken up with Mr. Cheever's defense of himself against the allegation of political preaching, because he denounced slavery, pointed out the national sin of which they were guilty, and declared that it would bring down on the land that tolerated it the judgments of heaven; and showed, by an appeal to the Old Testament prophets, and especially Jeremiah, that the same charge could be brought against them as had been brought against him; for Jeremiah, in the most emphatic and indignant terms, denounced this very sin of man-stealing, man-selling, and slaveholding, on its first entrance systematically into the land of Israel and of Judah, as filling up the cup of Judah's iniquity. Dr. Candlish quoted from Dr. Cheever's work in illustration of this, and also for the purpose of showing that Dr. Cheever held no extreme views in regard to the sin of slaveholding, in the sense that he would make no allowance for any circumstances that might hinder a man from getting rid of the possession of slaves, but who, at the same time, were not regarded or treated by him as such, but that his statements in this respect were singularly cautious, candid, and charitable. He also referred to the address sent by the General Assembly of the Free Church of Scotland to the Presbyterian Church of America in 1846, on the subject of slavery—the views of which, in substance, corresponded with those of Dr. Cheever, said that the reply of the American Presbyterian Church was to the effect, that they would beg them not to trouble them any more about this matter; and returning to Dr. Cheever's book, said he believed they had in this book a conclusive proof that no such a thing as slavery—nothing approaching to a man stealing another and holding him as goods and chattels—existed in the nation of Israel down to the very eve of the Babylonish captivity, when the institution of slavery filled up the measure of Judah's iniquity. For that service they owed Dr. Cheever inestimable thanks. The system that prevailed among the Jews was not a system of buying and selling men; it was a system of a man purchasing a man for himself, and for a limited time, and nothing more; and there was nothing in the slightest degree analogous in it either to man-stealing, or to man-selling, or to slaveholding, the sin with which America was chargeable at this moment; and those who were standing up to denounce this great national sin deserved the sympathy of the community of Great Britain.

Evidently matters are coming (said Dr. Candlish) to a crisis in America. Talk as they may about the risk of the Union being dissolved, most plain it is that the parties of the North and the South, the free and the slave parties of America, must now either come to an understanding, or they will be met by an earthquake or volcano. I do not find that Dr. Cheever advocates any very extreme views, even as regards abolition itself. The stress of his book is against the iniquity of those laws and proceedings that tend to defend and extenuate slavery. So far as I recollect, he refers to abolition much in this way—that if there were proclaimed a law that after fifty years there, should be a jubilee, as there was in the land of Israel, great good would be done. Of course, I understand, that Dr. Cheever means this, that he is clear for a law for proclaiming a jubilee at the end of fifty years, when all should go forth free; but he is for instant, immediate abolition, as much as I or any man could be who advocates immediate abolition. [Cheers.] He would instantly abolish any thing like a right to sell or buy men—any thing like a right to disqualify men from entering into the domestic relations of life—any thing like a restraint upon the education of any man—any thing like interference with his civil rights, or that reduced men to mere goods and chattels. [Cheers.] All that, of course, must be instantly and immediately abolished; but what I undertand him to mean is, that if this were done instantly and immediately, there would be time for such a gradual preparation as would make the ultimate establishment of equal rights for all Americans a safe and practicable thing. [Hear, hear.] I don't for my own part think, and I don't think Dr. Cheever believes, that any thing of that sort is now practicable. I believe it has—as it was in the case of our own West-Indian colonies —come to be a question of now or never. [Cheers.] Instant and immediate abolition will be carried, or America is gone. Events are thickening; and I believe that the event that has been announced within these few days of the execution of John Brown, is the first blow of the axe that is to be laid to the root of the noxious tree of slavery. [Cheers.] I believe that that event—I know it, indeed, for I have evidence of it in the American newspapers—is raising men in the North, even those who were apt to be passive and quiescent —even those who had great doubts about John Brown's proceedings—is rousing them to a ferment of indignation; and in the very first meeting of Congress the two parties met—the party demanding inquiry of the North as to John Brown's expedition, met by the party demanding inquiry of the South as to the proceedings in Kansas. Let them meet, and let them fight it out! [Loud cheers.] Of that expedition of John Brown, which ended so fatally, I am not now to speak. Let every one remember, however, that that expedition is a fruit of the atrocities of Kansas. [Cheers.] There, John Brown was exasperated, if ever man was. There, by the loss of two noble sons, and by other inflictions too much almost for humanity to bear, this man was roused

—I had almost said roused perhaps to madness; but no!—all about his proceedings bear the aspect of calm, deliberate, temperate judgment. There is no bloodthirstiness, no desire for violence. There is simply a desire to emancipate some, more or less, of his poor oppressed fellow-men. [Cheers.] In the expedition he played a high game; and he has lost and paid the forfeit in the loss of his two sons and that of his own life. I am not here to discuss the question as to the expedition. One may ask of that terrible execution of John Brown: What less could Virginia have done—Virginia, backed as it was by the whole power of the United States? There is one thing I will state, namely: surely that man was entitled to be tried by the whole of the United States, and not by one particular province of it; it may have been law, but I speak of justice. But supposing that the State of Virginia could not do otherwise than execute John Brown, I would just say that in the same sense I would be called upon to admit of the days of old that, with the power held by Lauderdale and his crew, they could not do otherwise than execute Argyle, Guthrie, and the men who fought at the Pentlands. [Cheers.] And, then, if I am asked about the expedition, I would be very much inclined to say, that if I am to shrink from answering whether it was treason or not, whether it was defensible or not for men to rise, I must have shrunk in the days of old from the question put, under the pressure perhaps of the "boots," whether I condemned the rising of Bothwell Brig as rebellion and treason—yea or nay. [Cheers.] I am very much inclined to put the two in the same category, [renewed cheers;] and I would be as loath to condemn John Brown as I would be loath to condemn the rising of Bothwell Brig, [continued cheers;] and, therefore, I hold that just as the blood of these martyrs—martyrs for Christ's Crown and Covenant in these days of old, kept alive the spirit of liberty, even when the days were getting darker and darker, and ultimately insured the triumph of civil and religious liberty—so it is my firm and deliberate conviction that this first shedding of blood on the scaffold by the slave power, in the person of such a man as John Brown—a man of God, I say, sir, for all the evidence proves him to have been so—a man misled perhaps; but if misled, which I don't admit he was, he was misled by his compassion for poor, wretched, degraded men lying under the lash of the master, [cheers;] I say the shedding of this man's blood will rouse the spirit of liberty, and will keep it alive until slavery shall lie prostrate, as Dagon did, a stump before the ark of God, in the idol's temple. [Loud cheers.] And now my own impression is, that in supporting Dr. Cheever, we are supporting him in doing, in a thoroughly legal way, very much what John Brown attempted to do. If John Brown had succeeded in carrying off some 300,000 or 400,000 slaves to Canada, who would not have cheered him, and called him patriot and philanthropist? who would not have been glad to fall down at his feet, and hail him as his country's deliverer? [Loud cheers.] He did not succeed; but I will not on that account consent to his being denounced and slain as a murderer. [Loud and prolonged cheers.] Dr. Cheever is doing practically very much the same thing legally that John Brown attempted by the hand of force. Dr. Cheever is attempting, and attempting successfully, to rouse the consciences of men practically, in immediate connection with the discharge of their own duties as citizens, in relation to this enormous sin of American slavery. I trust Dr. Cheever's testimony will rally round him a noble band who will throw themselves into the same cause, and with the same cordiality and enthusiasm which he has manifested. If we had at this moment some dozen Dr. Cheevers in the Northern States of America—if we had some dozen ministers likeminded with Dr. Cheever, and working with equal energy in the cause—we might hope for a settlement of this great question without anarchy, division, or bloodshed; but if there be not such a body of men ready to rally round him, I really fear that the sore must go on, getting more and more exasperating, until nothing but the immediate interposition of God, or God leaving the nation to utter anarchy, and confusion, and bloodshed, will solve the deepening difficulty of this great question of slavery. [Cheers.] Dr. Candlish concluded by moving a resolution to the effect that the meeting concur in a resolution adopted privately, that there was evidence enough to show that Dr. Cheever had borne testimony against the sin of slavery, which had involved him in great pecuniary difficulties; and resumed his seat amid loud cheers.

The Rev. JONATHAN WATSON, in seconding the resolution, said, Dr. Candlish had done the work so clean, that he left nothing for him to say. A nobler display of British eloquence and of manly Christian sentiment than that to which they had just listened, had not been heard since the days of Dr. Andrew Thomson; and the speech of Dr. Candlish carried him back to his younger days, when they listened to the eloquence of Brougham, Buxton, Wilberforce, and others, in the British Senate, on this very subject of slavery, as it existed in their colonies.

The resolution was put from the chair, and carried with acclamation.

Dr. ALEXANDER moved the next resolution, and said it spoke for itself, and was to the effect that the fact of such a man as Dr. Cheever being thus situated, and for such a cause, was fitted to awaken grief and alarm in the minds of all friends of liberty, indicating, as it seemed too plainly to do, the prevalence, even in the free States of America, and throughout the religious community there, of views on the subject of slavery, and the duty of Christian churches and Christian men in regard to it, that are in opposition to the spirit of the Gospel, and lead to palliate and perpetuate a system which every right-thinking man must desire to see speedily and thoroughly abolished. [Applause.] In supporting this resolution, Dr. Alexander said, that Dr. Candlish had, in his able and exhaustive speech, gone so fully into the matter, that he had left little or nothing for succeeding speakers. What the meeting was asked to do was, to consider whether a man who was occupying the position of Dr. Cheever was to receive their support, or to be left to fall under the opposition to which he was exposed, not so much for any acts of imprudence which he might have committed—none such having been proved against him—but because of the position which he occupied in seeking to oppose and to do away with that tremendous evil which was now oppressing and burdening the United States of America. Dr. Cheever's position at this moment was not merely that of protesting against slavery, but it was the position of a man who had armed himself and had gone down to the arena to take slavery by the throat, and to fight it to the death. [Cheers.] And in consequence of the stand which he had taken, the attempt was made deliberately to starve him out of the post he occupied, in order to silence his voice in the city where he lived as the great opponent of slavery. It was in these circumstances that they felt themselves bound to come forward, and not only to express their sympathy with him, but also to send him such aid as they could, so that the pecuniary difficulties of his position might be overcome, and he might be enabled to maintain the post which he had hitherto maintained so nobly and so well. He (Dr. Alexander) entirely concurred with Dr. Candlish in thinking that, if there were twelve men or so taking the same position as Dr. Cheever took, not merely theoretically but practically, and willing to peril all upon the advocacy of this great cause, and to fight the monster of slavery to the very death, the anti-slavery question would assume a totally different position from what it had ever assumed in the United States, and that the grand settlement of it in a satisfactory way would not be far distant. [Cheers.] In the appeal which they were now making to the Christian public of this city and country on behalf of Dr. Cheever, he had a strong conviction that they were taking a step in the right direction; for in the post which Dr. Cheever occupied he had opportunities of doing immense good; and they were also helping forward a cause, the triumph of which would be one of the greatest benefits which could happen to the United States. He entirely concurred in the sentiments that had been already uttered on this subject; for he believed that slavery was the great blot on the escutcheon of the American republic; and that if that question were brought to a satisfactory settlement now, a prodigious impulse would be given to the great energies of that mighty people. Her eagle, which was now partly chained, would then proudly stand erect and free, and would soar in the atmosphere of her noble destinies without a fetter to retard her progress, and without a cloud to settle on her wing. [Loud cheers.]

Dr. GUTHRIE, in seconding the motion, said that, late as was the hour, he could not help saying that he heartily concurred in every thing that had been said by preceding speakers. I believe (he said) slavery to be the sum of all villanies; I believe it to be the origin of the worst evils that afflict humanity, [cheers;] and I entirely agree with that old Englishman, Dr. Johnson, when he proposes as one of his toasts—and although I am not in the habit of drinking toasts, [laughter]—I would be disposed to give this one, premising it by saying, under circumstances that promise success : "The next insurrection of the slaves!" [Loud cheers.] I hold that, by the honor which I render to Sir William Wallace, to William Tell, to the men who broke the Stuart yoke; by the honor which I render to our Covenanting fathers, who took to the field of battle rather than submit to tyranny; I am bound to render honor to the slaves themselves, if they can work out and fight out their freedom in America. [Cheers.] No man under God's heaven has a right to sell me, my wife, or my children; and I say that if a man seizes my wife or my children to sell them, I hold myself justified in using any arms which God may have given me to resist him to the very death. I premise what I have said, by observing that the rising against slavery is a matter of prudence and of Christian judgment, and that it should not be done if the end of it is only to rivet more firmly the fetters of the slave; but if there is a fair prospect of the slaves asserting and making good their freedom, they are as much entitled to rise against slavery and to resist it as are the Italians to resist the Pope of Rome. [Cheers.] I won't blink that question. I would so act if I were a slave; and I would rather go from the scaffold of John Brown, and stand before my God on the judgment day, than stand in the place of those ministers of the Gospel who put the lock of silence on their lips in regard to this matter in their pulpits. [Cheers.] I have been often asked to go to America; they've promised to frank me back and fore. I have the highest opinion of the United States of America. I think that the people of America are, next to our own, the noblest people under the sun; and it is because I love them that I wish this foul blot removed from their escutcheon, and that they would break the chains of the slave. I think, if that were done, it would be a happy day for the world when they march south to Cape Horn with their Protestant truth and liberty; but may God shut them up within their territories—may he never allow them to set a foot southward nor northward of the continent which they occupy, if they are to carry with them the accursed system of slavery. [Cheers.] I have been, as I told you, asked to go to America; and I will tell you the reason plainly and publicly why I will not go. If I went, I could not keep my temper, [laughter]; and I might have to meet the fate of John Brown for any thing I know. I could not go and see a fellow-creature—a little child or a woman—set up to auction to be sold, perhaps with a horse or a wheelbarrow; it would stir my blood, and I could not hold my tongue. I could not stand the sight of such things in the South; and there are things also in the North which I could not stand. I could not go into one of their pulpits, and see a large sea of white faces, and then behold some poor negro, in whose beaming eye, in the tears rolling down whose cheeks I see a loving heart towards my blessed Lord and Saviour, and who perhaps is a believer passing any in that house—I could not see that man standing in a corner, and professing Christians refusing to sit down with him at the Lord's table—the man who, perhaps, will go into the kingdom of heaven in the front of them all—these are things which I could not stand. Neither could I stand this in a railway carriage; some poor woman, whose misfortune it is, if it is a misfortune, to be black, and who, because she is black, is turned out of that carriage, and dares not set foot amongst her white-footed and proud oppressors. These things I could not stand; and, therefore, I have never gone to America. They may think there is little loss in that, [laughter;] but I never will, till they abolish slavery. [Loud Cheers.] I love the Americans. In the months of August and September I see the clergy of every denomination, and men of every profession. I throw open my doors to them, and I am never happier to see any than Americans; but I make it a moral duty, when they are breakfasting with me, to dose them on the subject of slavery. [Loud laughter.] And it has always seemed to me that, the moment I touch upon that subject, it is like getting near a man or woman with corny toes. [Roars of laughter.] Dr. Guthrie then briefly noticed the remarkable progress make by the United States since its commencement sixty or seventy years ago; referred to its noble school system, its churches, and its missionaries; and said it was his prayer that God in his providence might lead that great people to break the yoke of their slaves. The existence of slavery had led many to doubt the work of the revival in the United States; and the churches of America were at this moment upon their trial before the world. He then stated that his Kirk-Session and that of Dr. Candlish had resolved to have collections in behalf of Dr. Cheever; and he hoped that the other ministers and congregations of Edinburgh would adopt the same course, and thus let the Americans see they were in earnest in this matter.

The resolution was then unanimously agreed to.

The Rev. WILLIAM REID proposed the next resolution, to the effect that the present appeal in behalf of Dr. Cheever afforded a seasonable opportunity for bearing an emphatic practical testimony against American slavery, as well as for expressing sympathy with those who, on Christian grounds, denounced it, and suffer loss for so doing; and that it ought, therefore, to be promptly and liberally met. [Applause.] Mr. Reid read several extracts from Dr. Cheever's work, to show the testimony which he bore against slavery, and the state of the American churches in relation to it; and concluded by saying that he trusted that, not only in this city, but throughout the length and breadth of Scotland, contributions from individuals and from churches would be freely given in behalf of the cause which had brought them together.

Mr. DICKIE, in seconding the resolution, said, the addresses which they had heard to-day were well fitted to stir up their feelings, and to call forth a liberal response from the friends of the anti-slavery cause in all parts of the country.

This resolution was also cordially agreed to.

On the motion of Mr. BURN MURDOCK, a vote of thanks was passed to the Lord Provost, and the benediction was pronounced by the Rev. Mr. Cullen.

MEETING IN GLASGOW.

AMERICAN SLAVERY.

A PUBLIC MEETING on behalf of the Rev. G. B. Cheever, D.D., was held in the Merchants' Hall on Monday afternoon, March 19. There was a large and influential attendance. Bailie Blackie presided, and on the platform we observed, among others, the Rev. Dr. Buchanan, the Rev. Dr. Smyth, the Rev. Dr. Robson, the Rev. Dr. Robertson, the Rev. Dr. Taylor, the Rev. Dr. Lorimer, the Rev. Mr. Russell, the Rev. Mr. Knox, the Rev. Duncan M'Gregor, the Rev. Mr. Batchelor, the Rev. Alex. Fraser, the Rev. A. G. Forbes, the Rev. D. M'Crae, the Rev. Mr. Forrest, the Rev. Mr. Borland, the Rev. Mr. M'Callum, the Rev. Mr. Jeffrey, the Rev. Mr. Clark, Barrhead, the Rev. Mr. Blyth, Councillor M'Dowall, W. P. Paton, Esq., etc. The Rev. Dr. Eadie, Rev. Dr. Jeffrey, and others, were in the body of the Hall.

The Rev. David Russell opened the meeting with prayer.

The Chairman then rose and said:

LADIES AND GENTLEMEN: You are no doubt aware that this meeting has been called for the purpose of expressing our sympathy, and taking steps to aid in his present position an eminent minister of the United States—one who, though personally unknown here, is well known by his writings, and perhaps as well known here as in his native land—I mean Dr. Cheever of New-York. [Cheers.] This eminent man has been for some time past lifting up his voice steadfastly and firmly against the inactivity and complicity, to some extent, of the American Churches, of their Bible and Mission Board, and Tract Society. Believing that the system of slavery, as existing in the United States, is contrary to the whole spirit and tenor of both the dispensations of the Old and New Testament, Dr. Cheever has been steadfastly setting his face against it; and finding his arguments not readily answered, attempts have been made to silence him in another way—to place him in difficulties from the position in which his congregation may be, by the amount of debt that has been upon it, by the expense of their church's site in New-York. And to accomplish this end, many of his leading people have withdrawn and refused their contributions. He has appealed already to the Christian men and women and abolitionists of the United States, and not without success; but he feels that it is desirable that the weight should not rest upon them alone, and that he may safely come to the Christian men and women of this country, and ask them to aid in this great effort to continue his testimony against the system of slavery in the United States. It would be trenching on the ground of those who are to move the resolutions, were I to go into any details on the question. The speakers who are to follow are much better able to state the position of the question than I. I may just add, that while we are met to express our sympathy with Dr. Cheever, an opportunity will be at the same time taken of calmly but firmly lifting up our voice against that system ourselves—[cheers]—a system that recognizes no right whatever in the slave, ignores his evidence altogether in any case, whether against himself or others, that prevents his master setting him free if he were willing to do so, unless he carries him out of the State in which he has set him free. Altogether the workings of the system are such as that I can hardly conceive it possible that any man, professing the name of Christian, should at all subscribe to it or submit to it. [Cheers.] The Chairman concluded by stating that he had letters regretting their absence, from the Rev. Dr. Symington, the Rev. Mr. Arnot, and the Rev. Mr. Edmund. He called upon the Rev. Dr. Buchanan to move the first resolution. [Cheers.]

The Rev. Dr. Buchanan, Free Church, then rose and said: The resolution which I have been requested to submit to this meeting is in the following terms:

"This meeting is solemnly convinced that American slavery is contrary to the word of God, degrades the moral and religious principles of the slaveholder, wrongs and corrupts the enslaved, and is injurious to all the political, social, and economical interests of the State."

Before addressing myself to the subject of the resolution, I wish it to be distinctly understood that I am not here to vilify America. If it were the design of this meeting to turn the question which has brought us together into a mere occasion for casting stones at a great and noble country, I could have taken no part in such proceedings. [Cheers.] I love America. I admire the amazing energy of its people. Instead of grudging, I heartily rejoice at the distinguished position which its intelligence and enterprise and boundless activity have made for it among the nations of the earth. [Renewed cheers.] As a Christian minister, I feel deeply grateful for the invaluable services which its press has rendered to almost every branch of theological literature, and which its missions have rendered, in almost every part of the world, to the cause of the Gospel. Nay, as one of the Anglo-Saxon race — as being of the same lineage and language of the American people — I have ever been accustomed to identify their interests and their honor with our own. [Cheers.] Nothing, therefore, could be more strongly opposed to all the impulses of my heart than to utter a single word fitted to excite harsh thoughts or unkindly feelings towards America. It is my deeply solemn conviction, that whatever breeds discord between Britain and America, breeds danger not only to the best interests of these two mighty empires themselves, but to the best interests of freedom, of humanity, of religion, all over the world. What I have thus presumed to say in the outset of this meeting for myself, I am well assured that I may with equal confidence venture to say for every individual within these walls. [Cheers.] Instead of its being because we love not America, it is, on the very contrary, because we do love it, that we are this day to lift up our most earnest protest and remonstrance against American slavery. In using that sad expression, "American slavery," I have specified the subject of my resolution. It is upon that dark and distressing subject that I have now to speak. With this resolution in my hand, I am here in the character of an accuser of American slavery. The resolution constitutes the indictment which the callers of this public meeting have deliberately framed against that revolting system of human oppression. If I have had any difficulty in undertaking to plead the case which this indictment raises, it has not been from any doubt as to the truth of its averments, but solely from the sense I have of my incompetency to do justice, and especially within the limits to which I must confine myself, to questions of such weight and magnitude as those which my resolution embraces. Four separate and specific charges are here brought against American slavery—charges, any one of which were enough conclusively to condemn it, but which, taken together, can not be made good without branding it, in the judgment of every dispassionate mind, with infamy and abhorrence. My resolution affirms of American slavery, first, that it "is contrary to the Word of God;" second, that "it degrades the moral and religious principles of the slaveholder;" third, that "it wrongs and corrupts the enslaved;" and last, that "it is injurious to all the political, social, and economical interests of the State." I believe it will need little argument or evidence to satisfy this meeting that the first of these charges is really the fundamental one. Whatever is contrary to God's Word — contrary, that is, to the mind and will of that righteous Lord who loveth righteousness and hateth iniquity, must needs be contrary to all the best interests of man. The question is, Does American slavery violate that law ? In other words, is American slavery in opposition to the great essential principles of the religion of Jesus Christ ? I feel almost ashamed at the very putting of such a question. [Hear, hear.] It is surely both a startling and a humbling fact that it should have to be put in this nineteenth century of the Christian era. [Cheers.] What is the law of American slavery? and what, on the other hand, is the law of the Gospel of God our Saviour ? Place these two laws side by side. Look now at the one and now at the other, and say whether reason, conscience, all the instincts of humanity, do not cry aloud that not more opposed is light to darkness—that not more opposed is Christ to Belial, than the law of the Gospel, which is the law of love, is opposed to the law of American slavery, which is the law of the basest selfishness, of the grossest injustice, of the most intolerable tyranny. The law of God says : "Thou shalt love thy neighbor as thyself." And if any one, in the spirit of the proud and supercilious Pharisees of old, shall think to except the negro race from the sweep and range of this Divine statute, let him remember that "God hath made of one blood all nations of men to dwell on all the face of the earth." The negro is a man, and, therefore, does God's law bind the white man to love him as he loves himself. Is it to keep this law to treat him, not as a man but as a thing, as a mere chattel, as a piece of property to be bought and sold in the market like a brute beast, and all this without even the allegation of his having committed any crime? His color is his only crime. He has the same material form as the white man, the same bodily frame as fearfully and wonderfuly made as his, the same bodily senses and powers. He is possessed of the same spiritual and immortal nature as the white man, of a mind capable of the same high thoughts, of a heart full of the same moral sensibilities, of a soul which, redeemed and renewed by grace, may reflect as brightly as that of any white man that breathes the holy and blessed image of God. If American slavery were chargeable with nothing more than taking one man and treating him as I have described, the fact might well arouse the most indignant outcries against it. Have we not seen recently all Europe joining in one loud and vehement protest against the iniquity of the Church of Rome, in seizing and separating from his parents the boy Mortara? But what is such an iniquity to that of a system which robs of their liberty nearly four millions of our fellow-men, which drags children every day from the arms of their parents, and sells them like sheep or cattle before their parents' eyes, which tramples all domestic ties and all domestic affection, whether conjugal or parental, in the dust? [Cheers.] It is an insult equally to reason and to religion to affirm that such a system is, or can be otherwise than eternally and irreconcilably opposed to the word of God. For my part, I have no patience to argue, at this time of day, with any man who has the hardihood to maintain the contrary proposition. It is doing gross injustice even to the imperfect economy of Judaism, to allege that because it contained laws to mitigate the oppressions, and to restrict the limits of servitude, it is, therefore, to be held as approving and countenancing slavery. And as regards the fuller and more perfect dispensation of the Gospel, under which it is our privilege to live, one knows not how to deal with those who dare to drag it into the witness-box for the purpose of making it speak approvingly of a system which its whole genius and spirit emphatically reprobate and condemn. It is mere trifling with the question to split hairs about the meaning of a Greek word, or to twist and distort the counsels of apostles or evangelists, addressed to those primitive disciples who might be under the yoke of heathen slavery, into a Divine sanction for that iniquitous system itself. It was not the method of the Gospel directly to assail political institutions, however unjust or oppressive. That would have been only to create a state of things under which it would have been impossible, in such an age, for Christianity to live. The infinitely wiser and more efficacious method which it pursued was that of inculcating principles which, in proportion as they were understood and embraced, would inevitably reform those institutions, and introduce, in all the relations of human life, whether political, social, or domestic, the reign of that blessed kingdom which is "not meat and drink, but righteousness and peace and joy in the Holy Ghost." Christ, the Divine founder of the Gospel, taught us the golden rule of his kingdom, that whatsoever we would that others should do unto us, we must do the same unto them. Is it compatible with that rule to establish and enforce the law of American slavery? Would the American slaveholder wish to be treated as he treats his slave? to be deprived of his civil and personal liberty; to be driven to his work by the pleasant persuasion of the cart-whip; to be denied the wages of his own industry; to be led out to the market, stripped, handled, and turned round by even the most brutal purchaser, in the face of the crowd, like a bullock or a swine; to have his wife or daughter subjected to the same degradation before his eyes; to be subject any day to cruelties and indignities of the most galling kind, without the possibility of redress—would any slaveholder, I ask, venture to affirm that in upholding a system which allows all this to be done to his slave, he is only doing to others as he would wish that others should do unto him? The very supposition is monstrous. It is an infamous libel upon the religion of Christ to allege, or even to insinuate, that it has any voice but one of the loudest and sternest condemnation for a system so outrageously wicked. [Loud applause.] Those who maintain such a line of argument are doing their best, however blindly, to put shame upon the Gospel, and to play the game of its bitterest foes. If Popery, by corrupting and caricaturing the Christian religion, has made myriads of infidels in the Old World, it is not less certain that the same deadly evil is extensively wrought in the New World, by putting upon that religion the cruel odium of abetting American slavery. [Hear, hear.] It concerns our common Christianity that the American churches should break up at once and forever even the very appearance of that shameful and unnatural alliance, by proclaiming fearlessly before all the world that, wherever else American slavery may find support or palliation, it finds none in the Word of God. [Cheers.] But not only does my resolution say this, but it says a great deal more. It goes on to affirm that American slavery operates alike injuriously on the slaveholder and on the slave. It has been truly and beautifully said of mercy, that it is twice blessed—" blessing both him that gives and him that takes." And not less true is it to say of slavery—which is another name for selfishness and cruelty—that it is twice cursed—cursing, as it does, both the oppressor and the oppressed. To be a slaveholder is to be invested with irresponsible power; and he must be ignorant, indeed, alike of human history and of human nature, who does not know how fatal such power is both to its possessors and to its victims. In the case of its possessors, its tendency is to cherish all the worst feelings and basest passions of the human heart. To conceive or sketch the character which it seldom fails to produce, needs no aid from fancy. Examine the state of society in any slaveholding country, whether of ancient or modern times, and you will find the picture drawn to your hand—and that too often in colors so dark, and in form so hideous, that they will not bear to be described. The slave States of America present, as all the world knows, no exception to this rule. It is impossible it should be otherwise. Human nature being every where radically the same, like influences will give birth to like results all over the world. Indolence, improvidence, imperiousness, cruelty, impurity, are some of the rank growths which the system fosters in the heart and life of the slaveholder. It blunts all the better feelings of his nature ; it vitiates his moral sense ; it drives him to tamper even with the integrity of the Word of God. Of the truth of this painful statement, what could be a more convincing or more humbling proof than the fact that it has driven its advocates and upholders in America to have recourse to theories, both in morals and religion, of the wildest and most extravagant kind ? What has given such power and currency there to speculations denying the unity of the human race, and thereby subverting the authority of Scripture, and the whole scheme of redemption, but just the dire necessity of finding some plea, however desperate, to excuse the enormity of the slaveholding system ? What but the blinding and corrupting influence of that system is it which tempts even the free States of America to go on, from year to year, staining all the glory of their noble struggle for national independence, by enacting and enforcing fugitive slave-laws which would not be tolerated in the most despotic nations of Europe ? And if in these and in many other ways the system works such fatal effects on the slaveholders themselves, and on the nation at large, in as far as it makes itself a partaker in their sin—it needs not to tell how it wrongs and corrupts the poor unhappy slaves. We are told, indeed, that the slaves are contented and happy. If so, whence arise these gloomy suspicions and fears which haunt the minds of their masters ? Why are insurrectionary movements among the slaves of such frequent occurrence? Why does the white population of the Southern States ever and anon feel itself to be living, as it were, in the crater of a volcano? These horrible panics, and the cruel coërcive measures to which they continually lead, tell a tale not to be misunderstood as to the sense which the slaves themselves have of their deep and bitter wrongs. But even if it were otherwise—even if they were as satisfied with their condition as the friends of the slave system would have it believed that they are, what would it prove but this, that slavery had at length succeeded, by its debasing and brutalizing power, in rooting out of them that deepest, noblest instinct of humanity, the sense of right, the spirit of independence, the love of liberty?

> 'Tis liberty alone that gives the flower
> Of fleeting life its lustre and perfume,
> And we are weeds without it.

[Much applause.] Thank God that even American slavery has not been able to eradicate this sentiment from the bosom of the negro. [Renewed applause.] Much as it has done to darken his intellect and to deprave his heart, he still knows and feels that he is a man, and in the very recoil of his nature from the yoke that weighs him down, there is the hope and the earnest of that nobler condition to which he shall yet rise, when the day of his deliverance shall come, and when God shall undo his heavy burdens and bid the oppressed go free. [Cheers.] There is still another charge against American slavery embraced in my resolution. It proclaims that system to be "injurious to all the political, social, and economical interests of the state." On this branch of the subject, however, important and interesting though it be, it is not my intention to enlarge. I most firmly believe that in every one of the departments now specified slavery is working deep and deadly mischief to the American nation and people. At the same time, what concerns their political, social, and economical interests may reasonably enough be considered as belonging mainly to themselves. Having already, however, dealt with this question, on the higher grounds of morality and religion, I am not disposed to take up the controversy on the lower platform of those considerations which are of a merely material, social, or political kind. This only will I say—and no intelligent American who is not himself personally interested in the slave system will deny it—that slavery is not merely the reproach, but the peril of the American nation. It is emphatically the sore place of their body politic. It endangers, and will continue unceasingly to endanger, so long as it is upheld, every great interest of the State. It disturbs the peace of families, it agitates and inflames the public mind, it keeps one half of the country in fierce conflict with the other, it unsettles the very foundations of the Republic; it is the most formidable hindrance to the nation's prosperity in peace, and could not fail to prove its deadliest enemy in war. If we wished ill to America, we should wish nothing so much as that it should cling to this atrocious institution. Slavery is the wedge of gold and the Babylonish garment that is troubling the whole camp of the United States; for verily there is a God that judgeth in the earth. "If thou seest the oppression of the poor and violent perverting of justice and judgment in a province, marvel not at this, for he that is higher than the highest regardeth, and there be higher than they." Those Americans are the best and truest friends of their country who spare no arrows on this momentous subject; who will neither be bribed nor coërced into silence regarding it. I believe Dr. Cheever to be one of these intrepid and faithful men. I have read his book, *God against Slavery*, and if the powerful and eloquent discourses which it contains be a specimen of his mode of handling this great subject, I can say nothing less than bid him God speed. They are full of "thoughts that breathe and words that burn." He deserves the sympathy of every lover of truth and freedom. May the day soon come when he shall cease to have his present painful though honorable pre-eminence, by reason of his being lost in the crowd of like-minded men! [Great applause.]

The Dr. Robertson, United Presbyterian Church, said: Dr. Buchanan is entitled to a double vote of thanks from the friends of spiritual independence on this side of the Atlantic and on the other. [Applause.] I am very happy to see a meeting like this at the present moment, because I believe that the principles of civil and religious liberty were never so extensively diffused among our people as now. It is, however, as Dr. Buchanan remarked, rather disagreeable in connection with a movement of this kind, to find that we are brought into collision with those brethren we wish to conciliate, and then we must remember our position on a platform like this. Were I an American minister I do not say that I would have the boldness I have now assumed, and if the system of American slavery prevailed in this country, I do not know that I would be up to the mark. I would remind you of this that we may do justice to brethren there, though we must never forget that truth is truth and sin is sin, and must be condemned; and slavery, though it be supported by able and eloquent ministers of the Gospel, is a bitter draught, and is none the less bitter on that account. [Cheers.] The fact is, that when we look at the history of the world we discover that when man alienated himself from his Maker, he lost the very idea of the unity of the race, and soon after the conqueror and the powerful began to tyrannize over the conquered and the weak. Hence servitude commenced at an early period; and if you look into the subject, you will find that when God interposed under the Mosaic economy, he did so to ameliorate the condition of the slave, and gradually work out the abolition of the system. Dr. Robertson proceeded to show that the Jews, under the old economy, were required to instruct their slaves morally and religiously—to invite them to their national religious festivals. They were at liberty to claim protection against their masters; and they were set free at the end of every six years, unless they voluntarily entered into fresh engagements. Dr. Robertson then went on to show that even in regard to heathen slaves owned by the ancient Jews, their condition was very different from that of slaves in America, and there was a general emancipation in the year of jubilee. How different from American slavery; and how strange that we should find Christian ministers advocating the infamy! It is remarkable that when the Christian dispensation is introduced, the true idea of the unity of the race is restored to its proper place. Who can forget that most sublime of all scenes almost—apart from those in which the Saviour himself was personally interested — when Paul addressed the Athenians from Mars Hill! Athens never contained more than 30,000 free citizens, and is generally computed to have contained in the day of its glory 400,000 slaves. And here you find the apostle on that most interesting occasion, lifting up the idea of the unity of the race before these slaveholders, and telling them that God had made of one blood all nations of men on the face of the earth. [Cheers.] There was a stroke at the principle of the thing, at the very root of the system. For the sake of the three or four millions in slavery, for the sake of the planters themselves, their wives and children, for the sake of that great country, the United States, in all its interests, I desire that the present state of things may be speedily abolished. Let the Americans remember that it is righteousness alone that exalteth a nation. May the time soon come when the shackles of the slave shall be snapped asunder, when the red dragons of war shall be unyoked, when thrones shall be established on justice and encircled by freedom, when men every where shall live under free equitable laws, and the whole habitable globe will be enlightened and free!

[Much applause.] The resolution was then put to the meeting by the Chairman, and carried by acclamation.

STATEMENT OF DR. CHEEVER'S CASE BY REV. HENRY BATCHELOR.

The Rev. Henry Batchelor, Independent Church, moved the second resolution, which was to the following effect: " While appreciating the great service rendered by the American churches to the common cause of the Gospel, this meeting deeply laments their complicity with slavery, and unfeignedly deplores the connivance of the churches in the Free States at this direful evil; very sincerely sympathizes with any ministers or churches who may be resolutely protesting against this national sin, and especially rejoices in the Christian, manly, and faithful testimony presented by the Rev. G. B. Cheever, D.D., and most earnestly commends the appeal for pecuniary help during the struggle to the warm and generous liberality of the churches in Great Britain." The speech on the resolution was to the following effect:

With a resolution like this in my hand, it would be highly improper to pronounce an oration. I confess that the first impulse of every unblinded and uncorrupted heart is to pour a torrent of wrath on the whole iniquitous system of slavery. Indeed it is impossible to speak in a direct address on this subject, without rising to the eloquence of pity, and indignation, and shame. I rejoice in the manly and nervous eloquence to which you have listened from my reverend predecessors to-day.

But my resolution chains me to a speech of facts. The resolution expresses appreciation of the great service rendered by the American churches to the common cause of the Gospel. After what has fallen from Dr. Buchanan, it will not be necessary to enlarge on this portion of the resolution, except to say that this statement was framed in good faith, and is now reiterated with cordial sincerity. The resolution next deeply laments the complicity of the American churches with slavery. The following facts are the evidence: Amongst the Protestant Episcopalians there are 88,000 slaves; amongst the Presbyterians, 77,000 slaves; amongst the Baptists, 226,000 slaves; amongst the Methodists, 219,563 slaves; amongst other denominations, 50,000 slaves. Here you have a grand total of 660,563 slaves, owned as goods and chattels by the ministers and members of the professing church. Here should be mentioned the fact, that the following great religious societies refuse to treat slaveholding as a sin: the American Board of Commissioners for Foreign Missions; American Home Missionary Society; American Bible Society; American Baptist Missionary Union; American Baptist Home Missionary Society; American Baptist Publication Society; American Bible Union; American and Foreign Bible Society; American Tract Society; American Sunday-School Union; the missionary societies of the Protestant Methodist, Episcopal Methodist, and Moravian bodies, respectively. The American slave system steals, sells, and barters human beings, separates husbands and wives, parents and children; compels adultery, polyandry, and polygamy; declares all is sanctioned by the Word of God, and admits slaveholders and adulterers to the fellowship of the church. The Rev. H. W. Beecher, in his Harper-Ferry sermon, preached on Oct. 30, 1859, asserts: "There is no church, that I have ever known, in the South that bears testimony against these things. If ministers," he continues, "will not preach liberty to the captive, they ought at least to preach the indispensable necessity of household virtue! If they will not call upon the masters to set their slaves free, they should at least proclaim a Christianity that protects women, childhood, and household." The religious bodies in the South, in conferences, presbyteries, and associations have, in different places, established the following conclusions: "1. That slavery is an innocent and lawful relation, as much as that of parent and child, husband and wife, or any *other lawful* relation of society. 2. That it is consistent with the most fraternal regard for the good of the slave. 3. That masters ought not to be disciplined for selling slaves without (the slaves') consent. 4. That the right to buy, sell, and hold men for purposes of gain was given by express permission of God. 5. That the laws which forbid the education of the slave are right, and meet the approbation of the reflecting part of the *Christian* community. 6. That the fact of slavery is not a question of morals at all, but is purely one of political economy. 7. The right of masters to dispose of the time of their slaves, has been distinctly recognized by the Creator of all things. 8. That slavery, as it exists in the United States, is not a moral evil. 9. That, without a new revelation from heaven, no man is entitled to pronounce slavery wrong. 10. That the separation of slaves by sale should be regarded as separation by death, and the parties allowed to marry again. 11. That the testimony of colored members of the church should not be taken against a white person—the church imitating the crimes of the legislature. Finally, it is practically admitted to be "right and proper to put down all inquiry upon this subject by Lynch Law." A minister of the Gospel has been known to exclaim: "Serve him right." These facts are surely sufficient to justify that very gentle word in the resolution, "complicity" with slavery. The resolution "unfeignedly deplores the connivance of the churches in the Free States at this direful evil." The history of the American churches presents a lamentable spectacle of progressive submission to the power of slavery. The connivance of the Free States is sufficiently exemplified in the cowering unfaithfulness of the great religious societies. For years the clergy in high places have been silenced by popular intimidation, and in some cases have become the apologists of slavery. The venerable Dr. Samuel Hanson Cox, whose face I well remember seeing in this country some years ago, is a notable example. Between the years 1833-38 New-York was agitated by slavery riots. Dr. Cox and H. G. Ludlow honorably distinguished themselves by giving the weight of their public position to the side of freedom. But the pro-slavery mobs smashed their church-windows, and dragged out the church-furniture, and flung it into the gutter. Dr. Cox has been dumb ever since, except as the apologist of the strong against the weak. The passing of the Fugitive Slave Law in 1850—one of the most daring enactments of slave policy—has anew stung the friends of liberty to exertion. This nefarious measure, which I need not stay to describe, was received by the majority of the clergy in guilty silence, and by not a few with still more guilty acquiescence. Hear the opinion of Judge Jay, one of the few of uncorrupted conscience, on this piece of pro-slavery legislation: " If you ask my opinion of the 'binding force' of this law, in a *moral sense*, I answer that its binding force is precisely the same as was that of the law of Nebuchadnezzar, commanding the multitudes the plain of Dura to fall down and worship the golden image—of the decree of Darius, forbidding prayer to God for thirty days—of the order of the Jewish magistrates to Peter and Paul not to speak at all, nor to teach in the name of Jesus—of the commands of the Roman Emperors, that Christians should cast incense on the altars of idols—of the edicts of Louis XIV., requiring the Huguenots to embrace the faith and practice of the Church of Rome. This accursed statute requires us to become *active* instruments of treachery, cruelty, and oppression, to the persecuted but innocent fugitive—to set at naught the law of Jehovah, to do justice and love mercy—to trample under foot the great commandment of our blessed Redeemer, to love our neighbor—and, regardless of His authority, to do to *others* what would fill *our* souls with anguish if done to ourselves. Let us, with our families, enter the dungeons which Northern politicians have prepared, rather than hazard our souls by rendering obedience to the requirements of this wicked law." But what said the clergy of the Free States? A few uttered indignant truth. The great majority were silent. But some proclaimed what one can not read without grief, and mortification, and shame. Bishop Hopkins, of Vermont, asserted that slavery is "warranted by the Old Testament," and inquired, "What effect had the Gospel in doing away with slavery? None whatever." Dr. Taylor, an Episcopal clergyman of New-Haven, asks: "Is that article in the Constitution contrary to the law of nature, of nations, or to the will of God? Is it so? Is there a shadow of reason for saying it? I have not been able to discover it. Have I not shown you it is lawful to deliver up, in compliance with their laws, fugitive slaves, for the high, the great, the momentous interests of those [Southern] States?" Do you wonder that infidel organizations against slavery denounce slavery and the Gospel in the same breath? Nothing but miracle could prevent it. Rev. W. M. Rogers, an orthodox minister of Boston, says: "When the slave asks me to stand between him and his master, what does he ask? He asks me to murder a nation's life; and I will not do it, because I have a conscience—because there is a God." A conscience! Delicate creature! He continues to affirm, that if resistance to the "Fugitive Slave Law" should lead the magistracy to call the citizens to arms, their duty is to obey; and, "if ordered to take human life," to maintain this unnatural enactment, "*in the name of God to take it.*" The Rev. Dr. Spencer, of Brooklyn, New-York, published a sermon in defense of the

"Fugitive Slave Law," which Dr. S. H. Cox highly lauded. Dr. Joel Parker, of Philadelphia, asks: "What are the evils inseparable from slavery? There is not one that is not equally inseparable from depraved human nature in *other lawful* relations." Dr. Gardner Spring, the eminent Presbyterian clergyman of New-York, protested in the pulpit: "If by one prayer he could liberate every slave in the world, he would not dare to offer it." Exquisite conscientiousness! A gentleman in Edinburgh was in New-York some time since, and attended the church of Dr. Spring. The portion of the word of God read was Isaiah, chap. 58. When the Dr. came to verse 6, "Is not this the fast which I have chosen? to loose the bands of wickedness, to undo the heavy burdens, and to let the oppressed go free, and that ye break every yoke?" he skipped over it, and did not read it. The sensitive piety which restrained his prayer expurgated the inspired word of God. Last, and not least—I can not tell you with what lamentation I announce it—the illustrious Moses Stuart, of Andover College, declared that, "though we may *pity* the fugitive, yet the Mosaic law does not authorize the rejection of the claims of the slaveholders to their *stolen or strayed property.*" How came the great Hebraist to confound voluntary, rewarded servitude amongst the Hebrews with *American slavery?* And how came he to forget, that the runaway servant was forbidden to be delivered to his master by the Mosaic Law? Rightly averred Albert Barnes, the commentator, one of the very few faithful ones, "There is no power *out* of the Church that could sustain slavery *an hour*, if it were not sustained *in* it." I think that this gentle word "connivance" requires to be strengthened to guilty complicity. The resolution "very sincerely sympathizes with any ministers or churches who may be resolutely protesting against this national sin." We know that there are such. All honor to them. The resolution "especially rejoices in the *Christian, manly,* and *faithful* testimony presented by the Rev. G. B. Cheever, D.D." The first thing to be done is to define Dr. Cheever's position. He takes this ground, that slaveholding is contrary to the word of God. This is the conclusion of all British anti-slavery advocates who are unmistified by the direct or indirect influences of slavery. I yield my hearty concurrence to the noble and stirring sentiments uttered on this platform. Dr. Cheever, simple man, requires that *sin* should be *treated* as *sin*. And why not?

Why should commercial dishonesty, drunkenness, unchastity, etc., be treated as sins, and not slaveholding, which is worse than any, and often includes and provokes all? Dr. Cheever demands honest, straightforward, church-action regarding this sin. He insists that political action should be as direct and sincere. If we want a Reform Bill, or the Repeal of the Corn Laws, we have an outspoken and hearty constitutional agitation about it. Plenty of ministers and churches call themselves anti-slavery people, but all they do is to remain silent, or very occasionally blow off a little pent-up talk which is not at all intended to be followed by practical action either in Church or State. Dr. Cheever is simply consistent. In the second place, I must sketch Dr. Cheever's course. In

1850, when the "Fugitive Slave Law" was passed, Dr. Cheever assailed and denounced it. When the Kansas atrocities occurred about 1854, and the slave party were bent on obliterating the landmarks of freedom by revolutionary violence, he, in like manner, invoked the condemnation of the Word of God. When the Dred Scott decision was pronounced, which excluded the testimony of a man of color from every Court of Justice in the land, and placed 4,000,000 of human beings under the heel of the dominant population, he lifted up his voice with the same energetic consistency. As you would expect, great dissatisfaction was felt in 1850. As the pastor "fulfilled his course," the grumble of opposition grew louder and louder. In 1855 the discontent broke out in open rebellion, and ever since the usual means have been plied to induce Dr. Cheever to resign his charge, or to eject him from his pulpit. I must, in the third place, show that Dr. Cheever's uprightness is the reason why he stands alone in New-York. I am not unaware that there are brethren in New-York whose hands are clean, and who are not implicated in the sin of slavery, even by connivance. But there is no man in any position of public influence who has made the thorough-going stand of Dr. Cheever. [Cheers.] In many large and fashionable churches in New-York the wrongs and the rights of the slave have no mention in prayer from year to year. Conniving clergy would not pray, and conniving communions would not hear. Ministers can scarcely retain their charges when they make a thorough stand against slavery. Nine clergymen, in one way or other, have been turned out of their pulpits since 1856, for uttering an honest testimony against slavery. They are these—the Rev. M. D. Conway, Washington, Columbia; the Rev. Dudley Tyng, Episcopal Church, Philadelphia, for one sermon against slavery, 1856; the Rev. T. B. M'Cormick, Presbyterian Church, Indiana, Presbytery of Cumberland, for aiding fugitive slaves, the prosecution being set on foot by his *clerical brethren*, 1856; the Rev. W. Sellers, tarred and expelled the State; the Rev. Samuel Sawyer, of Rogersville, for giving evidence against Colonel Netherland's brutal outrage on his slave, 1857; the Rev. J. D. Long, Episcopal Philadelphia Conference, 1857; the Rev. Moses M. Longley; the Rev. J. B. Boardman, for the utterance of free speech, 1856; a young Presbyterian clergyman, last summer, for preaching two sermons on slavery in New-York. The last would have stayed and braved opposition, but his church session, who admitted the righteousness of his course, advised him to resign. To these must be added — the Rev. Chas. H. Malcolm, Baptist Church, Wheeling, for refusing his name to a commendation of the ruffian who attacked Senator Sumner in 1856. [Loud cheers.] You will observe that a large number of these cases evidently occurred in the Free States. To further illustrate the difficulty of Dr. Cheever's position, you will find it asserted in an official document, lately issued by Dr. Cheever's church, that one or more of the Board of Trustees affirmed, " that the church must go down, and further remarked that, in his opinion, no thorough anti-slavery ministry could be sustained in the city of New-York." Henry

Ward Beecher confesses, in his Harper Ferry sermon, Oct. 30, 1859, that "the churches in the north," that is, the Free States, "will not, as a body, take upon themselves the responsibility of bearing witness against the enormities of slavery." While the Cheever demonstration was being held in Edinburgh, Dr. Cheever was being burnt in effigy near his own church, by a pro-slavery mob. [Cheers.] In the fourth place, I can not pass by the question which is so often proposed: "How is it that Dr. Cheever is so assailed, and Henry Ward Beecher is so popular?" It is an ungracious task to compare the merits of two anti-slavery advocates in my own denomination, and attempt to strike the balance between their claims. My feelings shrink from the duty, but my conscience demands that it be done. These ministers differ in opinion. I do not find in Mr. Beecher's opinions the thorough-going anti-scripturalness of slavery, and the radical sinfulness of any such relation amongst human beings. [Loud applause.] Next, these gentlemen differ in their public teaching on this question. Mr. Beecher blazes out now and then in indignant paragraphs, and at irregular intervals, as in the Harper Ferry sermon, preaches a whole discourse against it. Dr. Cheever has systematically elicited the revealed mind of God on the whole length and breadth of the immense iniquity. Moreover, Dr. Cheever watches and criticises the course of public events, and tries every new legislative evil in the balance of inspired truth. The "Fugitive Slave Law," Kansas monstrosities, Dred Scott decision, etc., each in consistent succession has been examined and rebuked. I saw in a New-York paper that Mr. Beecher had not preached on slavery for some fifteen months before October 30, 1859. He exposed, like Dr. Cheever, the criminal Fugitive Slave Law, Kansas, etc. After the passing of that ruthless statute, the Southern planters resorted to the most unscrupulous measures to silence all opposition. About 1852–53 a document was sent from slave-masters requiring the principal firms in New-York to sign an agreement to abstain from anti-slavery agitation, on pain of losing their patronage. I am informed that only a few houses withheld their signature. The terms of the stipulation, so far as I know, have never got into print. The establishment of Bowen & McNamee is honorably mentioned as having spurned the indignity, retorting: "No, gentlemen; we sell our goods, not our principles." Whether the dissatisfaction which was experienced in 1850 by Dr. Cheever was shared by Mr. Beecher, I know not, but clear it is, Dr. Cheever holds on his consistent though troubled way. Mr. Beecher is thought to be not as much given to out-spoken denunciation as in 1850, etc. I have not been able to ascertain that Mr. Beecher canvassed the Dred Scott decision, but have been assured that he did not.* Whether he is unconsciously yielding to the pressure of the slave-power time will not be long in telling. Further, these clergymen differ radically in their lines of practical action. Mr. Beecher demands no thorough, direct, and immediate action either in

---

* Since the meeting, I have been informed that Mr. Beecher *did* preach against the Dred Scott Decision.

Church or State for the overthrow of slavery. The Harper Ferry sermon is entitled "The right and the wrong way about slavery." I should be sorry to breathe a word against the many wise and noble sentiments, and just and indignant rebukes, which may be culled from the discourse. But its deficiencies are immense. Mr. Beecher discourages, as "a wrong way," the introduction of discontent among the slaves from without. How can we agitate for their freedom, and not awaken interior discontent? If we could, what could be more undesirable? If no discontent could be excited among the Negroes, then we had better let them alone. [Cheers.] They must be brutes, not men, and all anti-slavery effort is nugatory. Our duty is to tell slaveholders and slaves the right and the wrong of the whole business, and leave the truth to carry out God's laws to all their Divine issues. Mr. Beecher has six points on the "right way," neither of which attempts to plan or organize any practical action against slavery. His terrible fifth topic, on the "right of chastity in the woman, the unblemished household love, the right of parents in their children," I daresay has not been followed up by any urging of ecclesiastic or political action. Dr. Cheever is not content to deliver his conscience by firing off one well-primed topic on a theme so fearful, and then let the audience forget the flash of righteous anger and the thunder of righteous denunciation. [Hear, hear.] Once more, Dr. Cheever and Mr. Beecher differ in the societies to which they give support. Permit me to give you some account of the American Tract Society at Boston. Its principles are announced in official addresses, resolutions, reports, and publications. " We are not an anti-slavery society." " Not to be an abolition society." " Resolved, that the political aspects of slavery lie entirely without the proper sphere of this Society, and can not be discussed in its publications ; but those moral duties which grow out of the existence of slavery, as well as those moral evils which it is known to promote, and which are condemned in Scripture, and so much deplored by Evangelical Christians, do undoubtedly fall within the province of this Society, and can and ought to be *discussed* in a *fraternal* and *Christian* spirit." The poisonous root of all the evil is not to be touched, but some of the pernicious issues are to be *discussed* in a *fraternal* and *Christian* spirit. Imagine a grave committee, lay and clerical, *discussing* the rending asunder of all divine and human bonds, and the anguish of bleeding human hearts ; husbands, and wives, and parents, and children ; the shameless violation of wedded love; church membership and adultery ; in a *fraternal and Christian spirit*. What in the world is the work of a Christian Tract Society if slavery is to be excluded from its rebukes ? This trimming and treacherous society is sanctioned by the eloquence of Henry Ward Beecher. Now, let me place before you some account of the " Church Anti-Slavery Society" at Worcester. Its preamble, constitution, and declaration of principles avow its nature and objects. " The utter destruction of that atrocious system of Chattel Slavery which is maintained in the United States." " The duties of the officers and committees shall be . . . . to induce *action* by the Churches with reference to slavery, and to inculcate the duties of civil government, of civil rulers, and of citizens, in respect of *its overthrow.*" The word of God our charter to freedom, and our armory against slavery. " The system of American slavery, and the practice of slaveholding is essentially sinful and Anti-Christian, and *to be dealt with therefore as such by Christian churches and ministers.*" " No *compromise* with slavery allowable, but its total extinction to be demanded at once, *in the name of God.*" Dr. Cheever is a prominent advocate of this Society; Henry Ward Beecher has refused to speak at its meeting. Suffer me to direct your attention to one more society. I mentioned just now amongst the conniving organizations, " The American Board of Commissioners for Foreign Missions." The Cherokee and Choctaw Mission stations, it is well known, are in gross complicity with slavery. You can readily believe that the most revolting features of the slave system will be visible amongst such half-civilized tribes, and the guilt of the Board is the greater which tolerates it in its list. Now, the missionaries of these stations, as well as their church-members, are slaveholders. Just lately the Choctaw station has been separated from the Board, but the Cherokee mission is still supported by its funds, and shielded by its countenance. At the beginning of the present year, 1860, a discussion took place in Plymouth Church, Brooklyn, of which Mr. Beecher is the pastor. The debate created great excitement, which extended over five nights. The discussion was raised by some who held sounder views on the question of slavery than the pastor, and the resolution of the thorough-going Anti-Slavery advocate was to the effect, "That this church contribute no more money to the American Board, etc." On the fourth night of the debate, with all his influence, as the pastor of the church; and his unquestioned ability as a debater, Mr. Beecher supported the following positions, in a speech more than two hours long: "That the American Board was the proper depository of the contributions of Plymouth Church for Foreign Missions; that the Board had, to an unparalleled degree, kept pace with public sentiment on the subject of slavery; that it now held Anti-Slavery doctrines, and had faithfully and consistently applied these doctrines to missionary work; and that its record on this whole subject was clean, clear, and pure." Mr. Tilton, one of the members of the church, replied in a masterly address, which must have occupied two or three hours in the delivery, to the positions of the pastor. I recommend you all to read it. I must confess that I think the disciple is above his master. The speech of Mr. Tilton is a good set-off to the timid and compromising policy of the clerical editors of the New-York *Independent*. Mr. Tilton, I believe, is connected with the editorial department. Mr. Beecher is a warm defender of the American Board; Dr. Cheever, with characteristic consistency, moved, at the last meeting of the Board in Philadelphia, the following temperate resolution: "That, in the opinion of the Board, the holding of slaves be pronounced an immorality, inconsistent with membership in any Christian church; and that it ought to be required that these Missionary churches should immediately put away from themselves this sin, and should cease to sanction it even in appearance." Of course, Dr. Cheever's resolution was lost at the Board, and Mr. Tilton's in Plymouth Church. The pro-slavery journals, such as the *New-York Observer* and others, are exulting in the evidence which they think the tone of Mr. Beecher's speech betrays of growing conservatism on the question of slavery, and the friends of the slave are lamenting that his anti-slavery position is not more clear, unswerving, and strong. Fifthly. It is alleged that Dr. Cheever is intemperate and violent. It is all nonsense. [Hear.] Dr. Cheever does not hurl the scathing wrath of the Hebrew prophets, except when he quotes their Divine indignation, and is only as extreme and impracticable as the Sermon on the Mount. Henry Ward Beecher is as fierce as Dr. Cheever when he is in the mood. Only his is just an explosion and done with it. I have read Dr. Cheever's *God against Slavery*, his last thanksgiving sermon, and his lecture on John Brown, etc., and I defy any body to select invective as vernacular as the following in Mr. Beecher's Harper-Ferry Sermon : " Get timid priests out of the way, and lying societies, whose cowardice slanders the Gospel which they pretend to diffuse." The gentle Wesley called slavery the " sum of all villainies." Dr. Adam Clarke, in the coolness of the study, writing his commentary, penned : " How can any nation pretend to fast and worship God at all, or dare profess that they believe in the existence of such a Being, while they carry on what is called the slave-trade, and traffic in the souls, and blood, and bodies of men? O ye most flagitious of knaves, and worst of hypocrites! Cast off at once the mask of religion, and deepen not your endless perdition by professing the faith of our Lord Jesus Christ while ye continue in this traffic!" I remember no passage in Dr. Cheever like that. No, no; the hostility to Dr. Cheever is not to be explained by the charge of rash words. Slaveholding and conniving churches do not mind so much a few burning sentences. When they know that they need expect nothing more, they wince at the time, and all is over. It is when they dread *action* that they are aroused. Deep religious convictions, and calm, resolute, persistent exertion are the secret of retaliation. Society never troubles itself about hair-brained fanatics. They are always their own cure. The anger of Dr. Cheever's opponents is the proof that they know he is not mad. It is the impregnable force of his position, and the resistless grip of his argument which make them writhe. Dr. Cheever can not get a publisher for his last work in New-York. Nay worse, the Carters, who have published several of his books, dare not issue a neutral work on the sanctity of the Sabbath, which he has prepared for the press. Men are not thus frightened out of their propriety by the ill-temper of the insane. I have not much patience with this talk about hard words. For what is human language permitted to develop its keenest utterances, if not to strike down wicked things? There is no surer sign of benumbed sensibility, and of national declension in any special or general evil, than the prevalence of that squeamish euphemism which puts "*sweet* for *bitter*." Velvet adjectives must not clothe villainies. Every epithet for enormous iniquity ought to blister like a burning coal, and every sentence ought to be armed with the tail of a scorpion—all its startling pungency, but steeped in love instead of venom. There are some things so good, and some so bad, that they never ought to appear except in superlatives. To this latter class belongs slavery.

> O ye cold-hearted, frozen formalists !
> On such a theme, 'tis impious to be calm;
> Passion is reason, and transport temper here."

Sixthly, it is said that Dr. Cheever preaches perpetually about slavery, and nothing else. It is not so. I have seen it affirmed in his own church, that the ordinary range of Evangelical doctrine, instruction, exhortation, and comfort presented in Dr. Cheever's pulpit, has been quite equal in amount to that of any pulpit in New-York, during the period of Dr. Cheever's Anti-Slavery advocacy. [Loud cheers.] His set discourse on slavery are usually, if not always, announced before hand. Seventhly, it has been objected that Dr. Cheever's own denomination has done little or nothing for him. I believe there are some Western churches that have the disposition but not the ability to help him. The Western churches generally, which are the soundest on the question of slavery, are comparatively weak churches and largely dependent on the Northern and Eastern churches, and the latter are mainly conniving or pro-slavery churches. Besides, it is not to be questioned, that my own denomination is more deeply infected than it has ever been with the spirit of compromise. I am afraid that their honorable distinction in anti-slavery earnestness and consistency is being tarnished. Eighthly, I have heard it asked, "Why did Dr. Cheever build such an expensive church, and in such a position, to be burdened in this manner?" This is a difficulty very easily discussed in Glasgow. We are all fond of handsome and expensive churches. Gentlemen of wealth do well in raising noble structures for the service of God. Many of us have heavy ground-rent debts, etc., on our Glasgow churches. Suppose some twenty of the most opulent supporters of any Glasgow church, with their wives and families, were to withdraw, who amongst us, even if we had a good congregation remaining, would not be on the brink of church insolvency? If any of us were to drive away such a number of our people by pro-slavery preaching we should have to appeal to New-York to save us from bankruptcy. Ninthly, some have been perplexed how a church which lately sent $3000 to the Congregational Union for denominational purposes should be so easily embarrassed by debt. The explanation is easy. The conspirators would not give a fraction to the debt in most cases, because that would relieve the difficulties of the pastor, but they freely contributed to the Congregational Union. Several gentlemen gave $250 each for denominational objects, but would do nothing for the debt. Other difficulties might be stated and answered, but I have occupied far too much time. Permit me to say before I sit down, that I do not see, in looking over the field of the world, that we can do a greater or better work than to support Dr. Cheever in his position in New-York. We ought to raise £500 or £1000 for this object in Glasgow. It was never more important than now that we should make ourselves heard across the water on this question. People living in a great city can scarcely see the smoke which they are inhaling; but when you get a little way out into the country and look back, the dingy yellow stain dyes the blue sky with the sharpest distinctness. It will be of some service for Americans to know that we, who live out of the slave system, see as they do not the foul blot against God's clear heavens. When the olfactory organs are saturated with an ill odor, which breathed from day to day and year to year, we become totally unconscious of its presence. But our untainted senses revolt at the shocking evils of slavery. I fear—but I hope that I am wrong— I fear that the time for gaining a *hearing* on this question in the United States *has gone by*. In consequence of a long course of silence, and compromise, and apology, truth has lost its power to penetrate, vitalize and illumine. Unless I am totally ignorant of American affairs in Church and State, they have arrived at that terrible crisis when truth has become only a scorching and exasperating glare of condemnation. The history of a thousand nations proclaims that nothing remains to rectify the insulted laws of God and the injured rights of men, but judgment, desolation, and blood. [Hear.] The Americans are bone of our bone, flesh of our flesh, and blood of our blood, and surely are bound at least to hear us. Nay, we bought, at an enormous cost, the *right* to be *heard* by washing our hands from the terrible iniquity. [Cheers.] Let it go forth as the calm, deliberate, and solemn conviction of this meeting to-day that America can not flourish while slavery is gnawing away its moral strength, and marring its spiritual beauty. [Applause.] Let it be the prayer of every one that that country may yield to the quickening influence of the inspired truth of God, open like a flower to the light, and fling the hidden and pernicious worm forever from its bosom! The Rev. gentleman sat down amidst great cheering.

Mr. M'Dowell seconded the motion, which was carried with applause.

Rev. Dr. Smyth, Free St. George's Church, moved that a committee be appointed of the movers and seconders of the resolutions, to raise subscriptions. He cordially sympathized with the movement in favor of Dr. Cheever. In common with others, he had felt difficulties in consequence of rumors from New-York, and from quarters nearer home. But these had been removed by full explanation. He had been much gratified by the stand that Henry Ward Beecher formerly took, but he was sorry to find that he was retiring from that position, and leaving Dr. Cheever to fight the battle alone, on the sure ground which he had taken up. He could not trust himself to express the indignation he felt in regard to the complicity of the American churches in the matter of slavery. It was not humiliating that men who, in every other department of Christian service had approved themselves to God and their fellow-men, should, for any considerations whatever, occupy the position they still held in regard to American slavery. Dr. Smyth then referred to the unpleasantness of the duty he had himself to perform when, in company with the late Dr. Macfarlane, he denounced slavery thirty years ago, when a number of influential slaveholders belonged to his church, then St. George's Established, and added: Let us be charitable then to our brethren in America, and pray that God will give them grace to see how they are dishonoring him by their complicity with slavery. Dr. Smyth, before concluding, strongly recommended for perusal an Appeal to the Wesleyans on the subject of slavery, which had just been published.

Rev. Mr. Knox seconded the third resolution, which, like the rest, was carried by acclamation.

Rev. Dr. Robinson, in moving a vote of thanks to the chairman, which was heartily responded to, expressed in a sentence his sympathy with all that had been stated in course of the proceedings.

The Chairman, in acknowledging the vote of thanks, expressed his gratification at witnessing so large a meeting of the citizens at this time of day.

Rev. A. Fraser, of Ewing Place Church, then pronounced the benediction.

DR. GUTHRIE'S REPLY.

———•••———

To the Editor of "THE PRESBYTERIAN,"
Philadelphia, U. S.

Edinburgh, 27th February, 1860.

Sir :—In your paper of the 28th of January you have an article headed : " Drs. Candlish and Guthrie." Had that article appeared in any other than a religious journal, professing the highest orthodoxy, I would not have thought of noticing it, or of asking, as an act of simple justice, that you insert this reply. And, indeed, I am not so anxious to defend myself, as to seize the opportunity of lifting up my voice on behalf of the poor slaves, and of vindicating religion from the scandal to which it is exposed by your silence and that of others on the shame and sin of your otherwise noble country.

You say that "for my sentiments, temper, and language," at the meeting convened here to protest against American slavery, and to sympathize with Dr. Cheever, "there can be no apology." I will relieve you at once from any hesitation about accepting and inserting an apology by saying, that I do not write to offer one. Bad as, according to your account, my temper is, and capable as I am, in your opinion, of taking "leave of both of my senses and piety," it so happens that, much as I have been engaged in keen public controversies during the last thirty years, I have never yet had to apologize to any one ; and I thank God from the bottom of my heart that I have not now to go down upon my knees to any slave-breeder, slave-dealer, slaveholder, or to one I reckon more guilty than many slaveholders, one who, called to watch and give warning against crimes and sins, is, in regard to slavery, "a dumb dog that can not bark."

I write, not to make an apology, but to ask one. There are small charges in your article which are as untrue as they are contemptible—they are beneath my notice. So I pass on to statements equally false, but of a graver kind. You seem to have proceeded in this attack on Dr. Candlish and me upon "private information from an American gentleman." I presume your informer, the spy in our camp, is the person who was pointed out to me as a minister from the slave States. I beg his pardon if I am mistaken ; but if I have hit the nail on the head, let me tell him that it would have been more worthy of a gentleman and of a minister had he, instead of sneaking away to write a letter you have been too ready to believe, come forward to the platform like a man, and met us face to face. However that be, in your anxiety to damage, I do not say us. but any influence which our protest against slavery and its abettors might have, you have lent him a too willing ear, as I now proceed to show.

You state that I " spoke of the American eagle as polluted with blood." Now, that may or may not be the case; but I never used these words; nor said, indeed, a word, good or bad, about your eagle.

You state, also, that I wished the next negro insurrection to succeed, "though they might have to fight to the knees in the blood of the white man." How can I deny that? for in your article are not the offensive words, "fight to the knees in the blood of the white man," set within inverted commas, the usual sign of a quotation, and the pledge of accuracy? Alas for the credit of inverted commas and certain religious newspapers! There is not a word of truth in your statement. The wronged and down-trodden negro may or may not be justified in doing for his personal freedom what your own fathers did for their national liberty; though a man, he is black, and notwithstanding that an old-fashioned Book called the Bible says that God made of one blood all the families of the earth, he may no more have rights than the cow he is sold with; yet I never used the words, nor spoke of blood either on black men's knees or on American eagles. I felt confident, on reading your paper, that I had not employed the expressions you put into my mouth. Still, having a deep abhorrence of slavery, and feeling profound grief that such a system is allowed to live in such a country as yours, and that churches of Christ and ministers of the gospel have in so many instances failed to testify against it as they should, and God's old prophets would certainly have done, I thought it possible that my indignation might have exploded in some such terms. So I have appealed to the recollections of parties who were present, and I have carefully examined the report of the meeting in the three principal Edinburgh newspapers; and I have the satisfaction of informing you that neither the one nor the other give the shadow of a foundation for your charge. So, in the hope that henceforth you will be less ready to take up an evil report against your neighbor, and more slow in trusting to " the private information" of such " an American gentleman" as attended our meeting, I pass on to other matters.

You say that I was " blood-thirsty." A horrid charge to bring against any minister of the Gospel! If you mean, by applying this abusive language to me, that I delight in the shedding of human blood, or would have recourse to arms rather than suffer any wrong, I deny your charge; and appeal for my veracity to those who know me, and know how I abhor the cruelties inseparable from war. Perhaps you mean something else. Perhaps you mean that I would regard the slaves, if they had a fair prospect of success, as justified in rising to recover their freedom, and, as a last resource, meeting arms with arms in the battle for liberty. If so, I plead guilty to the charge; guilty, I must add, as were our Wallace and your Washington. Washington and his compatriots thought not liberty only, but independence even worth fighting for. In the days of the struggle which you yearly commemorate, ministers preached up resistance; pulpits as well as drums sounded to arms. You laud the men who did fight, and were ready " to fight to the knees in the blood of the white man," merely for the right to tax themselves, and have you the assur ance to hold up your hands in horror at the bare idea of poor Africans, ground to the dust, doing the same to save themselves, their wives, their children, from bleeding under the brutal lash, and being sold like cattle to the highest bidder? What were the wrongs your fathers suffered from Britain compared with the untold wrongs your slaves suffer on the same soil? Let the great Jonathan Edwards answer that question. He says: "We all dread political slavery, or subjection to the arbitrary power of a king, or of any man or men not deriving their authority from the people. Yet such a state is inconceivably preferable to the slavery of the negroes. Suppose that in the late war we had been subdued by Great Britain, we should have been taxed without our consent. But these taxes would have amounted to but a small part of our property. Whereas the negroes are deprived of all their property; no part of their earnings is their own; the whole is their master's. In a conquered state we should have been at liberty to dispose of ourselves and of our property, in most cases, as we should choose. We should have been free to live in this or that town or place; in any part of the country, or to remove out of the country; to apply to this or that business; to labor or not; and, excepting a sufficiency for taxes, to dispose of the fruit of our labor to our own benefit. But the unhappy negroes in slavery can do none of these things. They must do what they are commanded, and as much as they are commanded, on pain of the lash. They must live wherever they are placed, and must confine themselves to that spot on pain of death. So that Great Britain, in her late attempt to enslave America, committed a very small crime indeed in comparison with the crime of those who enslave the Africans." Your great Jefferson also speaks out his mind as strongly and as truly. "One hour," said he, "of American slavery outweighs whole ages of the oppression we rose against England to shake off!" You can not deny that; and though a violent termination to slavery is not one that any reflecting and right-thinking man would wish, the system, as one of cruelty, of immorality, of robbery, and of murder, is accursed both of God and man. It is the plague-spot of your State; the plague-spot of your churches; and should its end, which God forbid, be one of violence, on the heads of those who are not straining every nerve to bring it to a speedy and bloodless termination, will lie the guilt of all the fearful crimes that shall accompany its dying struggles. When these come, and the slaves are fighting for their rights, your disasters may recall the fearful words of Jefferson: "What attribute of Jehovah would allow him to take part with us?"

You sneeringly represent many of us as being "much more concerned for the slaves in the United States than for the degraded and wretched in their own land." Those who know us know that this is not true. Let me tell you that our concern extends to others besides the slaves in your country. Your informant concealed, or you have omitted in your article, all reference to the hearty admiration which I expressed for your countrymen and country—its greatness, its noble missions, its net-work of schools, its evangelical churches; but this ungenerous treatment shall not prevent me from expressing the deep interest we feel in the prosperity and character of your nation. Because of that, we are grieved to see the contrast between what is now passing in Russia and passing in the United States. Looking across Europe, we see a mighty despot, the head of a Church where the light of the Gospel shines dimly through many an error, bending his giant strength to break the chains of serfdom; while in free, in Protestant America, States are driving—shame to see it—innocent and free men of color from their territories; a man is sentenced to the gallows for no other crime than aiding, in obedience to the dictates of religion and humanity, a poor enslaved brother in his flight; and many, calling themselves free men and Christians, are seeking to restore the accursed slave-trade, and rivet the chains of bondage. The very report of these things makes our blood to boil. And when such things are done, many of you keep silence who ought to "cry aloud and spare not," while some wickedly and profanely attempt to justify them from the word of God. No wonder, when Scripture is perverted to such horrid purposes, that some abolitionists have been sent by the recoil over into infidelity.

Let me say, in conclusion, that no lasting peace nor true prosperity can be yours till the evil thing is put away. I believe that God will not continue to bless a nation which continues to maintain a system that is opposed to the religion of Christ, and tramples in the dust its golden procept: "Do unto others as you would have others do unto you." Without this spot, how bright your sun would shine! What a noble ancestry you had, and, rid of slavery, what a noble people you would be! Little did the Pilgrim Fathers who fled for liberty to your soil, expect the day when others for liberty would flee from it—in holds of ships, or by journeys in the dead of night, with the North star for their guide, and God for their protector, and bloodhounds on their track, glad to escape from a land that prayer and piety once consecrated to freedom. But we cherish the hope that, in the very confusion into which the question of slavery has now plunged your country, we see the "beginning of the end." We rejoice in the bold front, the onward movement, the increasing numbers, the growing power of the anti-slavery party. May God bless their banners, and speed on their cause, till, dark skin and white, your whole nation, amid universal rejoicings, hold a fast, even the fast that God hath chosen, the best evidence of a true religious revival, "to loose the bands of wickedness, to undo the heavy burdens, and to let the oppressed go free."

I am yours truly,
Thomas Guthrie.

www.ingramcontent.com/pod-product-compliance
Lightning Source LLC
Chambersburg PA
CBHW031609110426
42742CB00037B/1355